The Currency of His Light

poems

by Roy Beckemeyer

Copyright © 2023 Roy Beckemeyer
All Rights Reserved

Cover Photo: Roy Beckemeyer
Book and Cover Design: Rowan Kehn

Turning Plow Press

ISBN: 978-1-7355762-9-9

The Currency of His Light

for
the reader
who finds herein
a poem, a stanza,
a line, or a word
that seems to shine
with a different light,
that casts
an unlikely shadow,
that reveals some meaning,
some insight
that until now had
hidden like a shy mouse in
the unlit paths of memory,
its nose twitching with delight
at the thought of finally
being discovered

Appreciations

Writing poetry during the pandemic, political, and personal chaos of the recent past has been challenging. I and my poetry critique group companions Pat Beckemeyer, Julie Baker Brin, Dixie Brown, Judy Oliver, and Melany Pearce have flourished under the inspiring lead of Skyler Lovelace, who has kept us linked through weekly Zoom meetings. Clare MacQueen is Superhero editor and publisher of the online literary jewels *MacQueen's Quinterly* and *KYSO Flash*, and much of the work here has benefited from her keen scrutiny. Encouraging words from respected colleagues must be acknowledged; Thanks, Robert L. Dean, Jr., Arlice Davenport, Jeanine Hathaway, Caryn Mirriam-Goldberg, and Denise Low. I add to this list Paul Bowers, who, in addition to being writer and poet, is editor/publisher of Turning Plow Press. He and book designer Rowan Kehn have established a solid lineup of poetry, fiction, and creative nonfiction books and I am humbled to now have my work among them.

Praise for *The Currency of His Light*

Roy Beckemeyer, in his shining new collection of poetry, explores, questions, laments, and celebrates the mystery and power of light in language, art, spirit, and life. His deep and abiding investigation of the natural world generously gives these poems grounding, heft, and precision so that what's often beyond words can take flight. From murmuration at large to robins in particular, he brings what's often the backdrop of our lives into clear view, amplifying "the last August cicada saws" as well as the "Vidalia onion's dream." His homages to the arts and artists, including Monet and Milton in the title poem, reveals the sparks that make art, "…coined by eye and hand/ and light's merciless vicissitudes." Going deeper into mercy and its opposite, he writes of grief, love, and memory with startling tenderness, especially in the villanelle, "A Father Who Lives Longer Than His Son." Beckemeyer speaks intimately to the reader and his beloved, telling us, "You are the beguiling yin-ness / and yang-ness of mythology's shape changer," encapsulating in this poem how light is the ultimate shapeshifter. This whole book is an ode to wonder, and the kind of wonder we especially need to illuminate our lives right now.

   –Caryn Mirriam-Goldberg, Poet Laureate of Kansas 2009-13, author of *How Time Moves: New and Selected Poems*

Roy Beckemeyer's penetrating and beautiful new book of poems, *The Currency of His Light*, illuminates the wonders and mysteries of the natural world, the depths and hopes of seasoned love, and the power of his elegant poetry to enlighten and delight. These are poems to relish; they lead to myriad inroads of joy. And throughout is the light. At first blush, we notice how it quickens Beckemeyer's perceptions and poetics. In his expert hands, the vividly painted birds of the Kansas plain burst into a sharply focused new existence: They not only obey their nature, but they incarnate the poet's words, emotions, and meditations in their fluid movements over the fields. What's more, their avian glory is underwritten by the poet's imagination – the hidden fourth dimension of all things. With it,

nature blossoms into its full essence, encompassing the yearnings of our lives, as well. And for Beckemeyer, nature's finest demands poetry's best. And in this book, his best, he delivers. As with E. E. Cummings, love transports Beckemeyer's poetry to its rightful place between heaven and earth. The light shines on it, and beauty blooms from the shadows, sparkling with elevated diction, visceral imagery, keen metaphor and "the color of blessing." Highest recommendations.
  –Arlice Davenport, author of *Kind of Blue: New Poems*.

"Sometimes a piece of the sun burned like a coin between my hands." —Pablo Neruda

Contents

I
"When I consider how my light is spent,
Ere half my days, in this dark world and wide…"
—John Milton, Sonnet 19

Starlings—An Ode to Murmuration	3
Barbara Hamby Embraces the Swedish Word *Mångata*	4
Morning Thoughts of You	6
Light lies on water,	7
Hummingbirds	8
Rejoicing	9
The Way Light's Lapidary Light Burnishes Your Skin	10
Symphony Below the Threshold of Hearing	11
Autumn Poem	12
Robins	13
The Currency of His Light	14

II
"I don't paint people and things; I paint the way light reacts to people and things." — Harley Brown

Bedrock and Deluge	19
Alchemy	20
Pieces of Eight	21
Forever	22
Ugly	25
Palette	26
Argument	27
Sea Sprites in Flight	28
The pots	30
Wind and Walls	31
Aglow	32
The House Awakens	33

III
"I have seized the light. I have arrested its flight." —Louis Daguerre

The Color of Blessings	37
Perfection	38
Walking always goes forward…	39
Infinitesimal	40
Seppuku	42
Clarity	43
Hose	44
Auslese	45
Love Declared—A Sapphic Ode	46
Firewood	47
Whirl	48
August	49
Together— A Prothalamion	50

IV
"To light a candle is to cast a shadow." —Ursula K. LeGuin

Funereal	53
Metabolism	54
Thirteen Ways of Being a Shadow	55
Reprise	58
Poem Written on the First Anniversary of My Son's Death	59
Rust Belt	60
Countdown	61
Mark	62
Pyramidal	63
Chiaroscuro	64
When They Last Bloomed	65
A Father Who Lives Longer Than His Son (A Villanelle)	66

V

"Look at light and admire its beauty. Close your eyes, and then look again: what you saw is no longer there; and what you will see later is not yet." —Leonardo da Vinci

Declarative	69
After Leaf Raking	70
Sparks	72
Lexicon	73
Vidalia	74
Age Tries to Recall Youth's Departure	75
Multicellular	76
A Golden Shovel Poem	77
We All Breathe	78
Nature and Nurture	80
Shores	81
Prothalamion	82

VI

"There are dead stars that still shine because their light is trapped in time. Where do I stand in this light, which does not strictly exist?"
— Don DeLillo

Repose	85
Cold Spell	86
B&O	87
Don't	88
Evolution's copy editor…	89
Sanctification	90
Last Snow of Winter	91
Moments	92
A Simple Exercise	93
Suppose	94
Venus	96
Pilgrim	97

VII

"There are two ways of spreading light... To be the candle, or the mirror that reflects it." —Edith Wharton

Us	101
Discourse	102
Central Heat	103
Perception	104
Silverfish	105
At the Front of Class	106
The Prodigal's Siblings Speak	107
Hand	108
Barn Swallows	109
A Fish Stew or Two	110
Adjacence	111
Notes & Acknowledgments	113
The Author	121

I
*"When I consider how my light is spent,
Ere half my days, in this dark world and wide…"*
—John Milton, Sonnet 19

Starlings: An Ode to Murmuration

"The act of murmuring" states
Merriam-Webster, as if mutters
were actions to be taken, tactics
to be executed. Instead, I think
of scattered groups of Jewish
elders in Temple, bearded,
their intermingling voices rising and falling
like a wavering on oscilloscopes,
like radio waves of stars intermixed
so thoroughly galaxies become
indistinguishable, like the reverberation
of rumors welling up as low hums
from a thousand throats in crowds
in squares—anticipation, growing
expectation, gargled growl, white
noise of whispers, anguish,
hosannah, voiced or yowled,
rising like dust from the face
of dune, like bee swarm emerging
from tree hollow, like great flocks
of starlings in winter, cloud bank
of birds, black specks building
into breathing flexing organic
masses of sky seeming to be
searching for words, for some
way to articulate the feel of dive
and swoop and dervish, wing
flap and fling, each black dot
a separate consonant or vowel
seeking a way to join, to be voiced,
swelling lunglike with inhalation,
utterance made visible and nearly
intelligible by a great and ghostly
act of murmuration.

Barbara Hamby Embraces the Swedish Word *Mångata*

"…the Swedish word *mångata*…is the trail moonlight makes in
water. We can say it in English but it takes six words."
—Barbara Hamby

Each letter bobs and floats on the almost
imperceptible undulations of her poem's
scintillating surface, alternately mirrors
the moon's second-hand opulence
or basks in the rhinestone tawdriness
of the Milky Way, *a* trailing *t* trailing *twin-a*
trailing *g* trailing *n* trailing *å*, a train of barges
tugged by pilot-boat *M* so unerringly that you
must plumb the riverine depths of the word.

Mångata, you sing, vibrato bearing the sounds
from your mouth the way oxygen molecules,
whisked by protons, ride the curls
of the solar wind. Your lips poised,
you say the word again, set the phonemes
twisting into each line's gravity-wave ripple;
the word morphs into the poem in its entirety.

Your face is bathed by the high-altitude-
neutron-smitten charged red-particles
of oxygen molecules colliding; your cheeks
glow like a Swede's frost-bitten mug,
and you hold up your *nubbe* of *Akvavit*.

"*Skål!*" you shout, but the word that is
lambency skating the sea is *mångata*,
and the surface-tension glint of each brilliant
letter alternately turns toward and away
from the moon, tremulous, light-waveringly
alive, wave and particle doing a couple's
routine, a white-light wake skittering along,

a trail of your days laid behind you all the way back
to your beginning, documenting, in phosphorescent
shimmers, the moon's simultaneous revelations
of where you have already glimmered, of where
you have always known you were bound to gleam.

Morning Thoughts for You

In a world strewn with whisps
and whorls of galaxies that recede
in uncounted numbers, on
and on and on from every tiny
arc of angle in the glorious sky,

and where we stroll the earth
in our many multitudes,
each having grown from merest tiny
clot of blood to what we are today,

at this time when some among us
have learned to count
the code of coiled life and told
the teased-out secrets
of what it is we share
with mastodon, amoeba, bumblebee,

the ring and ting of the wind chime
just outside the door, the whisk
of wind that sets its tongue to work,
the fact that I awake again to hear
this plaintive melody call out
another morning of another day,

are each equally wondrous, I believe,
and worth preserving here,
in these few words, for you.

Light lies on water,

tries to nestle in troughs,
winnows froth at peaks of
combers, uses wave and particle
to enunciate gravity's undulations.
High alto twinkles and blue-gray bassoon
swatches of sea gyrate as breakers break
into rainbow's palette, billow reflections,
refractions, alternately bright then
mellow, catch at light, fracture it,
quiver with it, ripple it, skip it
like round stones that bounce
and glide until, momentum
consumed, they sink
into gravity's grasp, slip
beneath the bottle-green sea.

Hummingbirds

"Here are the gestures
of my hands. Wear them in your hair."
—Jane Kenyon, "Year Day"

The gestures of hummingbird wings
can be seen only by fellow nearly weightless
creatures, their prestissimo hearts, their
vivace wingbeats unobserved by us—slow-witted
slaves of time's viscous passage. Our massive
passivity, our image-smearing optic nerves warrant
that we will miss the flick of primary tip, the come
hither winding of wing path, the sudden flare
of flattened vanes.

To them we are forever living in slow motion—
are nothing but ridiculous stop motion *Gumbies*,
Wallaces, *Gromits*, *Lego Movie* characters,
more plastic than living tissue, beneath their notice,
unworthy of more than a millisecond of time,
worthy only of the same gesture Dietrich
might have used to dismiss Jannings,
a mere flick of finger, a *Blue Angel* blur, a tick
of an atomic clock, a gesture, a flick—
a lick without a hint of a promise.

Rejoicing

If I could, I would spread joy across your face
like wild blueberry jam and slabs of butter
slathered on toasted bread—the kind you'd eat,
then end up with face and hands sticky, needing
to be licked clean while you sat with giggling
friends and siblings on a sunny day in June
or July on Grandma's wide porch.

I would watch joy illuminate your face the way
your grandfather's bedtime stories did after
an evening of catching fireflies in jars —the way
those fairy godmother lanterns of blinking
exuberance magnified wide eyes on peering faces
painted by this flash and that shine.

I would speak to you of joy with words unfettered
from the page and swirling around as if they
were you as a child again—your father's
reliable hands holding yours in the centripetal force
of love's innate security.

I would sing you joy until it bursts from your throat
in robin warbles at sunrise, when shivering leaves
shimmer in sun dapples, or until it pours
as brown thrasher waterfalls from treetops
like breezes caressing children who romp
and scamper, limbs-akimbo, on sun-dazed grass,
who splatter May rain puddles with feet bare
as uncapped noggins.

I would bestow on you the joys of watching
your own children and grandchildren, nieces, nephews
and great-grandchildren experience for themselves
each and every one of the reasons you ever found
in this generous world for rejoicing.

The Way Night's Lapidary Light Burnishes Your Skin

"I shall whisper
Heavenly labials in a world of gutturals.
It will undo him."
—Wallace Stevens "The Plot Against the Giant"

The guttering candle sputters sibilant smoke streams lit by the flaccid lightning strokes of flame's last yellow out into mellow midnight; minutes lumber toward morning, roll like silent surf onto tomorrow's shore. I could articulate more: the moon's blathering light, the confusion and blare of this lunar luminance skimming the cursory surface of the world, the old owl-eyed orb towing the tide of Juno's hormonal opulence in through our window's gauze and gape. I sit watching candlelight lapping its lemon tongue against the contoured landscape of you, the moon silvering your dunes and dales, your plains and bays, and only wish to clammer on, to wade time's currents under the night's infinite inventory of illuminations, to watch your eyelids slitting open to solicit light—the candor of iris and lens, the receptiveness of rod and cone. You blink at me from the molten core of your soul— "Have you been watching me sleep again?" you whisper, and I, transfixed by eyeshine and light-seep and long, lingering habit, am once again undone.

Symphony Below the Threshold of Hearing

The opening strains of my symphony of silence would be white dunes sprawling toward the horizon's windless haze, the softening sunrise so still the shift of a single grain of sand touched by a scarab's claw would become cogwheel click against the mute, birthing dawn. Holding your breath, you would hear the Brownian motion of carbon dioxide paused in the passageways of your lungs as molecular tintinnabulation, and, as you looked up, the soundless advance of stars pulled across the sky by earth slowly turning to face the sun would swell into a crescendo of quietude.

Autumn Poem

If words fell like leaves in fall,
awhirl in constant motion,
skitters and curls of color,
scallop-edged, saw-tooth-rimmed,
succotash assortments of them,
think of the thousand ways
we might arrange them,
the paragraphs like drifts,
stanzas with lines
intricately locked, stem to
leaf margin, imbricate or
randomly layered words
ready to settle, to nestle next
to others of their kind, to make
up the rich tapestry
of dead leaves going back
to ground, to the disordered
anarchy of constituent bits
and pieces, to the earth-steady
cycles of water and air
and sunlight becoming
poetry.

Robins

The light reaches them first, there
in the topmost branches,
salutes tawny breast feathers
and night-black heads by
burnishing them with tangerine
glints of sun's initial peek,
unleashes their chorale,
their Dawn Unfolding, the way
Beethoven might have annotated
his score, singular woodwinds
scattered across the stage,
voicing the theme round
and round the neighborhood,
one from elm, another from hackberry,
then the tall sycamore
across the street, the wind-
canted silver maple that leans
over the fence. They braid complex
chords with one another, their
dual-noted syrinxes twisting
dancing thrush harmonies
that embroider narratives of fat
earthworms escaping rain-sopped
lawns along wriggling paths
through grass and mulch,
of nests holding sky-blue eggs
ovoid and flush full
of robin-in-the-making,
of countless trips from
branch to ground and back
again, of chasms of chirping,
bottomless chick-gapes,
and all the rest of coming summer's
short and endless toil and joy.

The Currency of His Light
(After Monet's "Houses of Parliament")

"When I consider how my light is spent…"
— "On His Blindness," John Milton

To gamble away light the way Monet did,
to chase its furtive peregrinations, to allow
it to slither through smoke and fog, skid
along the undulations of the Thames'
snakeskin surface at dawn, to crucify
another new canvas every half hour
onto the easel, to watch his own sweat
drip like blood from a criminal's nailed feet,
to dab pigments that capture light's
spatterings on the lenticular lens of his eye,
the first inkling of sight's failure: fog-within
drifting in counter-current to fog-without,
to scorch lips with cigarette, smoke trailing
a third stream of confusion across the view,
Houses of Parliament mere smears
of staid Gothic Revival outlines,
vergeboards and bargeboards lost to blur,
befogged, bedimmed, beclouded,
to lose the fractal infinity of detail,
the slabbed sameness of tiered arches
of limestone, to see as the hours progress
the kind of dissolution a hundred years
of acidic fog might wreak, to watch
stone become sun-molten: smoldering,
shifting, splodged, smirched, to map
color spaces with his LaPlacian brainstem,
to transform, to capture some small portion
of fleeting light and gradient hue,
transient as life's stain and blotch
on eon's forever un-finite span, the canvases,
leaning against the walls of every room,

snatched up in succession to replicate
yesterday's angle of sun and curl of smoke,
the artist minting with die and press:
planchet after planchet struck again
and again, coined by eye and hand
and light's merciless vicissitudes.

The Houses of Parliament (Effect of Fog), Claude Monet, 1903–1904, Metropolitan Museum of Art. Public Domain.

II

"I don't paint people and things; I paint the way light reacts to people and things."
— Harley Brown

Bedrock and Deluge

"Pack your throat with the stones a river depends on…"
—Ines P. Rivera Prosdocimi, "How to Swallow a River"

You are stone, I believe,
inexpressibly alone even though embedded
in the gravelly stream bed of your ancestry,
continuously withstanding the sinuous
deconstruction of history's meandering ways.

Yet again, you are the evocation of a deluge,
water swallowing earth embankments,
the chaos of spate and surge dislodging
stone and stability simultaneously.

You are the beguiling yin-ness
and yang-ness of mythology's shape changer,
shedding the stolid worker's bedrock steadiness
at shift-change to become River, voraciously
gnawing at every bound in sight.

Alchemy

"In the church of the art museum, you…
…breathe into your blood
the vintage ochres and crimsons
of dead genius."—Pat Daneman

From metal tube crinkled
and squeezed into a crushed form
like fungi or gnarled bark

come pigments redolent of urine,
of the toxic salts of cadmium
and mercury and lead, dabbed

and stabbed onto canvas
by supple hairs of sable
and squirrel, the artist's mind

removed by an arm's length,
a long-handled brush's extension,
from the picture's plane. Such

a tenuous connection, the wavering
arm, the subtle movement
of involuntary tremors, as if

the paint is placed by some spell,
some genius of precision,
of pigment touching as if directed

by wizard's wand, the darks and lights
and hues and tints turning
into what the eyes have always known

but were never able to imagine captured
anywhere but in the sinuous chambers
of memory.

Pieces of Eight

"…marooned upon the coasts of morning."
—Vassar Miller, "Bout with Burning"

I am a Gulliver, a plank-walking pirate,
and though this morning there are stars
to steer me by, and the tide of the day's
events glows there on the horizon
of streets and houses, for now
I prefer to be alone, a sole proprietor
of quiet shores, words my only companions,
thoughts my treasure map.
I listen, pace seven words east,
ten lines south, spy this small doubloon
shining on the sand.

Forever
(After van Gogh's "The Café Terrace on the *Place du Forum*")

"M. Vincent, peintre impressionniste travaille, nous assure-t-on, le soir, à la lueur des becs de gaz, sur l'une de nos places. [Mr. Vincent, an Impressionist painter, works, we are told, in the evening, by the light of the gas lamps, in one of our squares]"
— *"Chronique artistique et musicale"*, *L'Homme de Bronze*, Arles, 30 September 1888.

He arrives at *Place du Forum* as the Arles sky
pours its waning light over the precipice
of dusk. He had spent another day beneath
Provence's expansive brilliance. In Paris,
Lautrec had filled his brain with absinthe-
tinged anticipation of how southern light
became an inundating flood as the day
progressed, flushing fields and orchards
and blossoming trees free of all color,
sweeping those colors, awash in daylight,
down the sky like a waterfall over the horizon.

A full spring and summer of this
had been his and now September
worms its way into the alleys
and winding backways of his brain.
He must find how to brush these light-
drenched night skies onto canvas as well.
"I definitely want to paint a starry sky
now" he writes his sister, Wilhelmina.
"It often seems to me that the night
is even more richly coloured than the day,
coloured in the most intense violets,
blues and greens. If you look carefully
you'll see that some stars are lemony,
others have a pink, green, forget-me-not

blue glow."
He slides the tripod's weight off
his aching shoulder, stretches
and sighs, unfolds the slender legs,
taps them so that each stands steady,
wedged between the cobblestones
of *Pas du Palais*, takes up his palette,
the pungent odor of linseed oil
overpowering the aromas of coffee,
terrine of foie gras, drifting his way
from the warm glow of the café terrace.

Night descends quickly, and he lights
candles he has affixed to his straw hat,
becomes artist aglow, sees his pigments
with new eyes. "It's quite true," he writes,
"that I may take a blue for a green
in the dark, a blue lilac for a pink lilac,
since you can't make out the nature of the tone
clearly. But it's the only way of getting away
from the conventional black night with a poor,
pallid and whitish light, while in fact
a mere candle by itself gives us
the richest yellows and oranges…"

The waiters take orders, the diners chatter
and bite and chew and swallow away, glassware
clinks, knife and fork clatter against porcelain
and pewter. Passers-by ooh and ahh with delight,
chuckle at their good fortune to see
the artist at work at such a strange hour,
his red beard alive with candle glow and flicker.

"To the great delight of the café proprietor,
the postmaster, and those who love the night,
and to my own, I have stayed up
for three nights and slept during the day.

It sometimes seems to me that the night
is much livelier, and its colours intenser,
than the day," he would scrawl into
tomorrow's letter to his sister.

At last he steps back, inspects his canvas,
crosses his arms, nods, smiles. A busboy on his
way home looks over Vincent's shoulder,
then up at the sky. A prostitute steps out
from her doorway and joins them. She
has spent her working life on this corner
but has not seen till now what is all around her.
She too turns her gaze skyward. The night and
the stars have changed for them both—
for us as well, from this point,
for all time, forever.

The Cafe Terrace on the Place du Forum, by Vincent Van Gogh, 1888. Kröller-Müller Museum. Public Domain.

Ugly

He was ugly as ethnic cleansing;
his haunting Bergen-Belsen face,
his Zimbabwe eyes, set deep
as a mass grave bulldozed
to hold a thousand men condemned
for their skin color, their sect, whether
they were or were not circumcised;
starving children stumbled
from his face like crocodile
tears, his croc teeth pulled
them all under brown water
like limbs cleaved from antelope,
gnashed them, red and flayed,
from their humanity, left them
raped, gutted, dead as his soul.

Palette

"…white flower's perfection
hiding a rumor of pink
at its center…"
—Lori Brack, from "Dearest Little L"

A rumor of pink,
a hint, a crowning
birth of magenta; an allusion
to the existence of
another hue shackled
in a cellar, chained
and padlocked in its rude
cell; a forecast of mauve
arching through Earth's
particulate-hazed
evening curvature;
a twitch in the grass
that may be ochre
burnt or raw; a raw
feeling the exact shade
of blood within arteries
blurred by age-yellowed
skin; a bent note auguring
a denotation of all the tints
and despairs of blue.

Argument

Their arguing was like birds.
Sparrows twittering.

After all the years,
a nest egg of knowing—
each what the other would propose.
Or claim.
Or muster.

One or either
might as well abdicate.
Don't you think?
No matter.
It was all for the sake

of argument

Sea Sprites in Flight
(After John Anster Fitzgerald's Painting, 1860)

When the combers have calmed
and the moonlight claimed
the horizon once again

and the sea lies silver-scaled
as the sides of sardines
flip-a-flop on the deck
of a pilchard-fisher's boat,

then the nymphs of the sea
rise from the haze and swirl
the soft swards of the bay

and lift their arms
and sing with the surf
the tales of the sailors
and sea-faring men
who have slid into the deep.

As the moon entwines
and spritely wings swish and flash,
and the water slips up on the sands,
we gather there
to write their names once more
though each swell of the tide
lifts them back to the sea.

"For that is where they belong,"
the sea fairies chant,
with tongues that sound
of droplets and spume,

"here in the sea where her moods
remind their bones

of the wind in their eyes,
and the taste on their lips

of the green that can only be found
on a moonlit night after a storm
on the skin of the scrimshaw sea."

"Sea Sprites in Flight," by John Anster Fitzgerald, c 1860. Public Domain.

The pots

hang like metal bats from the kitchen ceiling, copper bottoms, stainless handles and bowls, mouths stretched wide with longing. Each prays for something to moisten its cavernous openness, to feel heat roaring up against flatness, to wrap that heat up and around what it might mouth: the glistening slick fat rending from meat, the luster of roux liquefying, the caramelized bits of onion becoming translucent, stews drenching carrot and bean and turnip with succulent sauce, rich broth. One dreams of napping, lidded, in the warm cave of an oven, a roast, brown and crusty engulfing pink tenderness, nestled in its belly. They share their hunger openly, watch for your reflection in their neighbors' sparkling mirror shine, each waiting for you to look its way, for your hand to reach for its hooked handle.

Wind and Walls

"A first blow that could make air of a wall…"
—Seamus Heaney, "A Shiver"

The first gust sweeps over a stone wall,
says "I can't budge you, so up I go,"
curls in on itself to lift leaves once
wedged on that far side lee, a flourish,
a grand gesture of sorts, braggart, loud-
mouthed dust-in-your-eye scion
of highs descending onto lows, of
Coriolis-Effect-spinning-earth meteorology,
calls out, "I'll be back in a month, bringing
rain. It's slow business, wedging you apart
with drizzle and freeze. I will rise again
just at that moment you convince your-
self I was of no consequence at all."

Aglow

"…children making paper planes
from the pages of hymnals…"
—Traci Brimhall

The paper of hymnals, slick,
thin, translucent enough
that sun-pierced stained glass
brings the pages to life—
tropical birds glowing
through cloud forest fog,
and you long to release the sheets
from their binding, fold
and crease them, send
them soaring, bobbing
on the exhalation harmonies
of singing churchgoers—
rollers and combers of breath
lifting these notes, these hymn-
bird flocks of praise,
heavenward.

The House Awakens

What is that sound? A snowplow mounds snow like cumulus!
Driveways blocked! Snow masks the sleepy facades
of houses. Children see the raised hand of Providence
in school closings, their laughter and shouts are canticles,

songs of life, hymns. Fitting, in this nearly entirely secular
city—snow bringing what Sunday once did: somnolent pulse,
calm, an almost holy light. "No school today!"—a homily,

a chant, a prayer. And parents quietly chatting—a homily
as well—these unhurried moments: Percolator pulses,
furnace wheezes warmth and benediction. Is this house secular?

A place of worship? Is there a difference? Familiar sounds: canticles
of the everyday, often missed. God is in the details, providence
in a child's snow-chilled hand. Children return, faces open facades
of joy. Blessings accumulate, mounding high, like cumulus.

III
"I have seized the light. I have arrested its flight."
—Louis Daguerre

The Color of Blessings

Blessings can be the rich, warm yellow
of gamboge, of the breasts of Baltimore Orioles,
of the flesh of Central American mangos,
although sometimes, blessings are the color
of the jaunty bonnet worn by a coppery
Caribbean girl walking heat-stricken
sands under a molten sun, or of ripe
just-peeled peaches dripping in the hands
of a cream-skinned Georgia belle.

Blessings may be more orange than yellow,
on occasion, especially when the recipient
does not deem herself worthy; then
they may glow like polished orange peel,
a textured, deeper hue than the fresh-squeezed
juice in the glass held by Miss Sunkist® 1957
as she swayed on the seatback of a gilded
ochre Cadillac Seville convertible.

Blessings can be ostentatious yellow,
sun-dried apricot yellow, the shade
of rayed Binney and Smith suns on third grade
What I Did Last Summer drawings, the color
backlit amberina vases become where amber
glides and glistens into scarlet.

But blessings are nearly always the color made
when the sun, streaming through the garnet-
stained glass of a rose window in a European
cathedral tints a gold chalice being raised
by an altar boy destined, two centuries in the future,
for sainthood.

Perfection

"Perfect English and perfect sense don't always go together!"
—Walt Whitman

You would perfect the English
of your poem, polish its syntax,
burnish each punctuation mark
until it gleamed, its intent intrepid:
stable tripod of clarity, concision,
congruity, solid of soul, masterly
metaphorical, meteoric, Mephistophelian
in its implicitly intricate simplicity.

Walking always goes forward in time,

whether the path goes left or right, uphill, around a curve. So start younger, time travel the only way you can, now that words and images have grown fuzzy, neural connections gone slack, brain full of corroded terminals, the static of loose wires: Take up a picture you don't really recall. But there you are, silver halide dissolved, and emulsions fixed. Your new tricycle smile, as if you just rode out the door and down the steps and are revving up to lay rubber all the way to today, legs lengthening, face elongating, ways being set in much the same way the image was fixed, becoming an adult, riding right ahead as if you had two capital letters in each name, as if you became Mr. *DeLorean* McFly on the fly, headed for the future straight as an arrow. Well, no more than a few twists and turns as you go, but after all, those just make the yarn tighter, pull the weft and warp into closer contact. Ponder: did you leave these sunny days behind soon enough, leave the lead there in the earth, the dust not settling as deeply into your lungs as it would if you had stayed? The

grass is still green, the house has not settled. You pull out a phone and raise it to your eye and tap the screen and charge-coupled devices and CMOS sensors dot pixels: red / green / blue and there is the house, the steps, and here, now, once again, are you.

Infinitesimal

"Body my house
my horse my hound
what will I do
when you are fallen"
—May Swenson, from her poem, "Question"

It falls to all of us,
invariable as gravity,
to decline precipitously
or with glacier-slowness,
or, blessedly for most,
at a steady yet always
surprising pace, this
weathering of all that arose
so long ago when sperm
pierced ovum—
that microscopic collision,
infinitesimal second orgasm
that no one really feels.

(Although, we knew,
when our second
child was conceived,
that the seed had sprouted,
knew before passion's
complete withering,
so perhaps that cellular
intensity is not always
beneath our perception.)

Why, then, the quizzical look
when first we discover
that we can no longer stand
on one leg to pull on a sock,
arise from one knee

without a handhold, read
the dosage instructions
on the pill bottle?

Body, product of mother's ovum,
father's lunging spermatozoa,
my cells greedily dividing,
my fetal fingerling,
my bawling newborn. Body my
crawling, my toddling, my striding,
body my sudden sexuality, body
my finest maturity.

Body my fixer-upper, my
unsafe dwelling, body my
scheduled-for-demolition hovel,
body my vacant lot. Body,
my once and fabled house,
reduced to this single, crumbling
foundation stone.

Seppuku

Moths, flutter-ghosts at lights,
dust-fling wings that are
their own shadows,
opening and closing
like Oriental fans,
the light's Geisha-allure—
white-faced siren bulb's
misleading glow—the Kabuki
theater of harsh shadow
and lurid slash, the sudden fall
from grace, singed and battered,
found by blackbirds
in morning's hungry light.

Clarity

"…notes
adults have trouble
hitting, holding"
—Kevin Rabas "Easy for Me"

Our notes of childhood
ring out clear and higher
than our post-pubescent
drones, sing, still, somewhere
across the dimensions
of time, out of synch,
now with the photon-
painted gold-toned movies
of our lives, the flurry
of image and sound
complicated sinewave
mixtures that refract
and reflect and sliver
through slits to devolve
into constituent colors
and notes pure as carefree
days where you and I
run through light bright
with promise, heads high
and voices brilliant
with the clarion-clarity
of youth recalled.

Hose

When I grew old enough to take notice,
women's legs, seamed and silk-smooth,
intrigued me. Those old *Look* and
Life magazines, newsreels, black
and white movies on late night TV
showed them, the line centered
on the backs of their legs. The way
they pulled them on, looked over
their shoulders into full-length
mirrors on door backs to check
alignment, as if those curves
could ever be accurately bisected,
the contours of women's legs
being so three-dimensionally
complex. Analytic geometry,
calculus, the nonlinear mathematics
of flesh, the topology of calf and
ankle and denier, the disappearing
trail of seam beneath swaying
pleats of skirt.

Auslese

"In the Moselle the sun
is a broken bottle of light"
—William Matthews, "*Wehelener Sonnenuhr Auslese* 1959"

Along the Moselle River sunlight
cascades downslope, breaks
like wavelets and tumbles
sparkling through twining leaves,
spots them with gold, dots them
with bubbles of warm light
that presage clusters of grapes,
fall's coming freshets of Riesling
and Pinot Gris, of sunlight streams
becoming tributaries of crisp white wine,
the river's ancient and yearly
second flood, captured in barrel
and cask and bottle to quench
the world's thirst for sun and slate and sugar's
soulful and leafy transubstantiation.

Love Declared – A Sapphic Ode

I wish her sweet face revealed each thought she thinks.
Love is what I seek. Unhidden. On display.
Each time she takes breath, looks up at me, she blinks,
quickly turns away,

hides her truth from all, as if she would not dare
show, ever allow love or even its hint
loose, would not speak first. I gladly thus declare
myself. Strike and mint

love's glittering coin. Astound them all, my bright
face lit like that gold, her eyes on mine aglow.
Love's flush, on her face, will not again take flight:
What I sought—bestowed!

Firewood

With fall's red arrival
we haunted the sawmill,
wraiths in search of leavings

from logs squared off
with screeching runs
through whirling steel,

each tooth taking its toll
in sawdust and the odor
of hot wood and scorched

sap. We lifted one end
of each slab onto the rusted
pickup bed, slid it, like a bow

across the steel-strung tailgate
viola, left three feet of wood
hang behind to wave and flex

with each pothole plunge,
each tarred rampart road repair,
all the way home.

Whirl

"…the wind blows nothing
but night"—Don Stinson

Some nights the wind
seems to move even the stars,
clouds scudding by them so fast

my point of reference shifts
and I float, too, the wind moving
the fine hairs on my arms

and neck as if it were me
streaming, swimming the sea
of sky, phosphorescent

constellations my wake,
the stars alternating blue
or red or white as they churn

and spin with each kick
of my feet, and I reach out
with my arms fully extended,

seize hands-full of air and light,
spend the whole night roiling, become
a cyclone of starlight and gusts.

August

"…thick night, prickled with drought
and dim stars…"
—Joey Brown, "Caroline, Summer Night, 1947"

You'd think these nights
baked to a deep brown
would be buoyant,
would bob above
the unevenly heated
surface of it all,
wouldn't just lay
like a blanket you
heave breath through
with effort, wring out
all the moisture you'd rather
hold in reserve, leave
dark stains beneath
your arms, salty
remnants edging
your cap brim,
prickly heat on the baby's
bottom. A sepia haze
dims the thin light of night,
the sleepy dullard stars
treading darkness
overhead.

Together – a Prothalamion

"…this is what we fear…
Nothing to love or link with"
—Phillip Larkin, from his poem, "Aubade"

And so, we come Together,
sometimes headlong, sometimes
hesitant, always wondering what,
at the heart of things, being together
rather than alone will entail. Will
there be ribbands, tatters, debris,
someday, splinters all that's left
once the wood of together is split?
The frigid steely ring of maul, of axe,
the grunt of the downward swing
the only wedding march, the only
dissonant, harsh song remaining?
Or will together be like driftwood,
first alive and growing,
swaying in wind, suckling
air through transient leaves,
sap ascending, seeds dropping,
sleeping the long months
of winter, stirring again in spring,
phloem the vessel of desire?
We choose to believe that, even felled,
 finally, by savage storm, hurricane winds,
swept to sea, grain swelling in
the welling surf, then tossed ashore,
together will be salt hardened, iron-
solid, cells linked, bound, forever wed.

IV
"To light a candle is to cast a shadow."
—Ursula K. LeGuin

Funereal

"…dressed in what you've yet / to live…"
—Jenny Molberg

You try on the morbid
blandness of casket couture,
approach the coffin, the
funerary vessel, the fine
jewel box of final remains.

You match the refined
understatement, the lack
of power tie, the failed
soft touch of pocket square,
hope your face is not as waxen,
unexpressive, glance down
to see how much of life appears
in how the cloth drapes,
how earth tugs it around
the living body, how unsettling
the image of suited man,
formally attired, but prone.

You try to make the transition,
the jump from vertical to parallel
with the ground in your mind,
try to imagine how you might look
if you were to trade places, look up
into the dark glass panel, and see it there:
your face, softening, slipping
back toward your ears, your lips
going slack, your collar bunching
up and almost imperceptibly
loosening just above the Windsor-
knotted, gray-striped, tie
of the deceased.

Metabolism

All our lives
our bodies burn,
consumed in brazen flames,
in slow smolders,
in alternating conflagrations
and sputtering acres of hot ash,
glow and flicker in the winds
of one another's passing,
smother and cool beneath
the blanket of being alone,
but always retain,
within our tinder hearts,
the spark our mothers
breathed to life, tended
so carefully
in their cupped
and shielding hands.

Thirteen Ways of Being a Shadow

I

You will have no name.
He will call you "my shadow."
They will call you "his shadow,"
or, if addressing him, "your shadow."

II

You will touch his lover's breast before his hand does.
You conform to her contours closer than his hand does.
You always come between his hand and her flesh.

III

In daylight you may lead him or follow him.
At night, his lantern will leave you behind;
he will drag you by your feet, your head
bouncing against stones.

IV

You were delivered with him from his mother's womb.
You will go with him into his tomb. If he is cremated,
your last appearance will be as a cloud's shadow.

V

You are infinitely flexible, climbing, wrapping,
extending. In medieval times men were racked
until they ripped, were drawn and quartered.
It was only then that their stretching shadows
were broken.

VI

He eats and devours as well the shadows of his food.
Who can know from which he draws more sustenance?
Stories from our shadowed past tell of being mired
in the dark reaches of a man's paunch,
his gut.

VII

You are often at your best when he is weak.
In hot sun you thrive, edges crisp, contrast strong.
He will sweat, overheat, gasp for breath,
then seek out your tree- or building-bound brothers,
bask in the respite they provide.

VIII

You stand upright only when he is near a wall,
a solid fence, a screen, a cliff face. You leap from
horizontal to vertical with ease, drop back equally
quickly, the ultimate fast-draw gymnast. He is
a dullard of motion by comparison.

IX

You will catch the shadow of a high fly ball
at the instant he catches the ball. If he fumbles
the catch, the ball and its shadow will high-five
each other as it bounces away.

X

When you lead him, he sees the way clearly,
when you follow he often loses sight
of what matters.

XI

When he leaps you will lose him
for a moment only. Never fear;
you will always meet him
exactly where he lands.

XII

Indoors are rooms with many lamps.
You will often see your other disparate but
constituent personalities. They will withdraw
back into you as one when you return outside.

XIII

When he retreats to the darkened cellar,
a room with blackout curtains,
a dank cavern where you cannot follow,
he may allow himself to perpetrate
what he cannot do in your presence.
You may in fact be nothing less
than his conscience.

Reprise

"…and gasp at our beautiful demise"
—Paul Bowers "Round Hay Bales"

May we go simply, quietly,
side by side, perhaps,
at least in the silent company
of those we love, knowing,
in the end, that it was
mostly good, mostly satisfying,
that we did the best we could,
or at least the best we thought
we could, may we go contentedly,
and, if not with a gasp, at least
with a sigh, if not a beautiful,
at least a comely, demise.

Poem Written on the First Anniversary of My Son's Death

Faces unfurled of masks, they gather *en masse*,
seem inured or ignorant of the ways of a virus
that seems to think for itself, that considers
how easily, while its hosts ignore it,
it can go forth and multiply.

And though it does not read; neither do
many of them. They do not listen, think
only of plots. They do not listen, believe only
in conspiracies. And when bodies are dropped
into open pit graves they avert their eyes.
No worse than flu, they say.

And then their leader nods and bobbles
shows them his way,
lulls them back to sleep.

Meanwhile, bodies have lain undiscovered—
all these wasted days when
not one of us thought
to think of them.

Rust Belt

All those moments gone
 to rust, to the red iron
oxide of indolence,
the corrosive lack of care,
the flaking-off
of any sense of commitment,
stain spreading like the dead stillness
 of abandoned steel mills,
the hulks of blind autos stacked
haphazardly along Ike's
Great Idea, the weedy fields
unmowed, where unseized initiative
slumps into obsolescence,
the fractured frame of wasted time.

Countdown

"I like the generosity of numbers.
The way, for example,
they are willing to count
anything or anyone"
—Mary Cornish, "Number"

Age is just a numbers game,
the long, slow, arduous
click click click of the pawls
as your roller coaster car
climbs through childhood,
the infinity of preteen years,
the aching anticipation
of high school and hormones,
then the summit, the peak
of life force and potential energy
that lasts for such a blindingly short
lightning strike of an instant,
becomes a maddening, stomach
churning race, the feeling with
each passing year
that you are about to fall
headlong out of your seat,
everything a blur, then, suddenly,
that sudden shift from negative
to positive g's, the bottom where
it is now all speed rushing to finality,
the fleeting end of the carnival ride of life.

Mark

"Grief settles in winter trees."
—Stephen Meats

Grief can settle in any season
even the height of summer's sun
a son can die before his father,
leave July forever a month undone.

Things grow and flower—colors flare,
but I now have one child instead of two.
Birds flourish—fledglings fill the air.
There should be more I could say and do.

Grief has taken root, I think, and will still be around
as Solstice approaches and leaves come to ground,
and will settle, I suspect, in the bare-branched trees,
to leave me numbly circumspect on days like these.

Pyramidal

"Pyramidal, Its Certain Form"
—Julian Talamantez Brolaski

Squatting on their plateau
surrounded by Giza City
they are blatant and yet
perfectly nonchalant
unlike at Tikal where
they peer at one another
over the trees, certain,
in their knowledge of blood
and sacrifice, that the same moon
will rise on priests and pharaohs
again as continents sail the Earth's
seas and civilizations churn out
new shapes to be built
and celebrated and found,
eventually, wanting.

Chiaroscuro
(After Caravaggio's "Sacrifice of Isaac")

Caravaggio saw this stark scene in black
and light: Abraham about to sacrifice
his life's blood, Isaac's throat in deep shade,
barely lit. The artist led by luminance's glare
against stark background's intense gravity,
where light waves wither, like grapes
on phylloxera-infested vines, at any distance
from the central scene, to light only an angel's face,
his hand, a lamb, Abraham, blade in hand, visage
clouded with dim, reflected light as much
as fierce grief, his son's bare back lit blindingly
in his father's view. We draw the triangle
in our minds: Angel hand on lamb to Abraham's
hand on Isaac's head; his father's arm, shoulder,
bald pate; Angel's head down his arm and back
to his hand; find unexpected stability, sudden
calm, the tense readiness to obey God's instructions
trussed up, restrained by God's relent, His nearly remiss
mercy.

Caravvagio. *Sacrificio d'Isacco*, 1603. Public Domain.

When they last bloomed…

"When the kitchen is lit by lilacs…"
—William Matthews, from his poem, "Familial"

Lilacs last a short time,
bloom outside
the back door, weep
violet-blue tears
of racemes, light up
the blue and red cones
of our daylight eyes,
every panicle a miracle
we use to tally the state
of our souls.

A Father Who Lives Longer Than His Son (A Villanelle)

A father who lives longer than his son
learns truths he wishes now he didn't know:
the novel ends before the tale's begun.

The bet is lost before the race is run,
rivers, it seems, from seas to mountains flow,
for fathers who live longer than their sons.

The blackest sky at noon, then midnight sun,
the wheat is harvested before it's sown,
the novel ends before the tale's begun.

Death dispensed by prayer, blessings from a gun,
rock-steady man who wavers to and fro:
the father who lives longer than his son.

The sun-burnt man has never seen the sun,
the catcher-caught fly ball was never thrown,
the novel ends before the tale's begun.

The weightless waif who weighs more than a ton,
the immigrant who never left from home,
the father who lives longer than his son
whose novel ends before the tale's begun.

V

"Look at light and admire its beauty. Close your eyes, and then look again: what you saw is no longer there; and what you will see later is not yet."
—Leonardo da Vinci

Declarative

What if I declared my love to you
on a frigid morning in January?
I could stand, the sun at my back
beaming its impressions of warmth:
yellow and red skitterings of light
peeking through branches.

We would have on earmuffs
and woolens. You might wear
your stocking cap. Your cheeks
would be Braeburn round, reddened.

My words would take on whole
new meanings, visual onomatopoeia;
you would see me in a new light.

The heart-ring shape of the word
"love" would spin out of my mouth
to become ice-rainbow. Your name
would float into bright air, the cold
draping each vowel and consonant
with crystal luminance.

My whole proposal might hang
in mid-air, linger long enough for you
to send a "Yes" out into the space
between us, the sibilance trailing off
like a contrail, barely tethered between
your teeth, the mingling of our breaths
sparking and scintillating, a flock
of miniscule white birds released
from a suddenly opened dovecote.

After Leaf Raking

My eyes are drawn this morning to branches bare of leaf,
and to the sky beyond.
Leaves skittering make such a soothing sound—
amid such music, knee-deep in a sheaf
of leaves that blow and skiff and flicker
like a wind tossed flame. I shed gloves and cap and slicker,
kick off my boots and dive headlong
into the smell—these leaves that wind and sun have set alight,
breaststroke, frog kick, swim the song
of scuffing leaves right down the street,
leave my neighbors gasping at the sight—
a slow old man suddenly become so swift and fleet.
I hold that thought, keep my council for my own,
though such ideas well
up again and again, an oceanic swell
of autumn feel. Tell
me that you understand, that I am not alone
in celebrating autumn's last hurrah,
honoring leaves that lived overhead,
letting them know that we remain in awe.
Let our eyes, green with envy, set the tone,
admire the gold that's left once green has been forsaken,
these sunstruck colors where October's path has led,
this last flourish before old winter stirs,
his breath of frost saying he's awakened.
And summer's given up all that was hers
to claim, to this upstart time of change,
for green has worn our eyes with trying
to catalog the myriad summer shades of leaves now dying
in a burst, a bed of glowing coals the wind arranged
into this array of jigsaw puzzle pieces—
it all ceases:
everything that ever took a breath
turns in the turn of days to rubble,
contributes to the compost heap,

disintegrates in the depth
of winter's hold, brittle stubble
of fields an old man's beard
of lifeless gray.
Harbingers, these leaves, of what we feared:
the steep descent of what was on its frigid way,
set to arrive some night while we, the heedless, sleep.

Sparks

"Where are my bees, my hornets, my dragonflies,
long-coated Toscaninis in black tie and tails…"
—Barbara Hamby, from her poem, "Ode to Insects"

The last August cicada saws
away at the day's waning light,
scratches at carnal romance's
primitive rhythms.

The last firefly of September
tugs his lantern along the dark
weedy avenues of evening,
blinking arias of unrequited love.

A dust-gray moth lifts from grass
fast losing its green to nightfall,
the colorless simplicity of moth
now recorded in eggs clinging to
these final themes of summer's receding.

Lexicon

"…somewhere
someone speaks in a tongue I will never know"
—Kevin Rabas, "Translation"

Speaking this wordless language
of decades and seasons,
shared glances and barely
perceptible smiles,
brushings in passing,
looking up from a scene
to see it imprinting in each
other's cascade of memories,
knowing we are both
descending that staircase,
lifting left feet over the same
scuffed patch of carpeting,
relaxing our fingers' grip
at that splintered bit of railing,
seeing the sun spattering through
leaves into the dark corner
of the stairwell, opening
the door through which
we stepped together,
that first time, so many
years ago, when we inscribed
the initial entries in love's lexicon
of lives lived long together.

Vidalia

"…Carrots and potatoes
that will hang like stars in my deep
bouillon dark."
—Pat Daneman, "Soup"

Vidalia onion's dream:
to be translucent, to be
butter-glisten, shred or dice,
free from rings heart-ward
and skin-ward, lit
by stove light sky,
adrift in Pinot Grigio sea's
heady embrace, afloat
on lines and skeins
of bubbles in a twisting
and rolling and diving
synchronized swim.

Age Tries to Recall Youth's Departure

Age collects in those pouches under
your eyes—age and forgotten hours

collaborating, swelling translucent skin bags
the way pails fill to spilling with what drips

from maple spiles, all the sweetness
of life thinned nearly to its own watery

essence of absence. Other parts of the body dry,
husk-like and fragile as will-o-the-wisp,

skin that has its own rules for folding
and draping; resilience, no longer subcutaneous,

gone missing, that certain inherence
to become supple, to burgeon, has slid away

unseen, unnoticed, in some quiet moment
between midnight and dewfall as the body

rolled in sleep's surf and surge, while youth,
its limberness and ability for renewal, drifted off

on one or the other of time's relentless equatorial
currents, its first tentative, languid breast strokes

alternating with slow, lazy crawl, each stroke
more urgent as the body fell further behind.

Multicellular

"Your body is a science
experiment—all hypotheses,
no promises."
—Pat Daneman, "Time Remaining"

You grow from single cell
to what you are the day you die
in stages poorly understood,
cells dividing according to
instructions coiled onto
strings of proteins mankind
struggles still to read,
signaled by potions,
by stringent codes of here
not there by logic devices
illogical in execution,
by mistake, by precise
adjudication, by what
you can only see as evil
intent or loving beneficence,
debilitating symptom or heirloom
of succulent grace.

A Golden Shovel Poem
(After Li Po's "Drinking in Moonlight.")

I lean back, tilt my chair, and so
sit on just two rickety chair legs,
with two weak and wary legs of
my own for tenuous balance, see
wine-red sky as I stretch to look, the door
ajar—the view framed aslant, perspective
among the other strange aspects of this scene,
flowers pinked by the reddening sky,
blossoming in twilight filtered through
trees, looking like cloned blood moons.
"No," I say to the dog, "still a bit early, though
one might decide blood-moonflowers are
to die for, glowing in all their glory. I'd
drink to them, toast them each
with my rarest vintage, burgundy deep red and
well attuned to sinful sunsets, but
there's time yet for us to wait;
the ivory light will soon take over—
moon's light—the bright bone-moon kind."

We All Breathe

We breathe in time with our mothers;
we are small moths at their milk-flower breasts.
We breathe in polyrhythm,
one breath for each five heartbeats.
We breathe in—lungs unfurling like time-lapse
images of blooming hydrangeas.
We breathe in, speak out
in myriad tongues.

We all breathe.

We breathe raucously—first breaths
bursting from aquarium wombs.
We breathe haltingly, guts sucker-
punched by fear.
We breathe lavishly, savoring lovers'
exhalations.
We breathe guiltily, watch confessors' eyes
blink, then widen.

We all breathe.

We breathe out the way stampeding stallions
raise haboobs to stun the desert's sun.
We breathe out the seawater spume
of the nearly drowned.
We breathe out crystalline clouds,
the wage of winter's reign.
We breathe out, accordion ribs shrinking
like street musicians' squeeze boxes.

We all breathe.

We breathe through masks meant to confuse contagion.
We breath at distances that allow

our plumed breaths to wither between us.
We breathe through ventilators—our lung sounds,
machine-like, hiss and skirl.
We breathe in unison for those who took
their final breath alone.

Nature and Nurture
(After Betsy Sholl's "Genealogy")

Her mother was a terrarium, her father a plinth.
She pried stone apart like wild honeysuckle.

She saw them cross her dream as adornments:
fuchsia and hologram, diesel and feverfew.

One of them was syncopation the other a caisson.

Her myth was iconic as an iron lung;
the liana reflected in its mirror became the motif
of a traditional *Eṣfahān* rug.

One of her parents was an hourglass counting sands,
the other rattled hooves against the drumhead of her mind.

One of her parents she blew across the lawn like
dandelion seeds, the other she enshrined as a curio.

In the loom on which she was woven, one of them
tied off her warp ends, one left her frayed.
Thus, her aphasia, her jaundice.

One was arsenic, the other attestation.
How they debated mortality's flavor.

One was burette, the other kelp. She was consumed
by her own spare metrics, sustained by offshore abundance.

She was a girl braided into the floor of the earth,
always overshadowed by what loomed overhead.

Shores

Those first few times,
fumbling fingers tentative, yet
urgent to decipher the lexicon of lover's
braille, to map the stratigraphy of layers
of clothing, to undo the impediments
of hook and eyelet, of snap and zip
and button, to skim the expanse of sultry,
silken skin, to skate finger pads along
winding paths of exploration, over swell
and swale, approaching, receding, promising,
withholding, sliding, almost succumbing,
conducting the duet of each other's breaths,
the whispered entreaties, the twinges,
the breathless affirmations, the lifting into,
the engulfing, the steeplechase heartbeats
stretching beyond the final turn
into the straightaway, neck and neck,
each desperate to discover with the other
all these untrodden shores.

Prothalamion

"By this light the salty fishes / Arch in the sea like tree-branches, Going in many directions / Up and down."
—Wallace Stevens, from "*Homunculus et La Belle Etoile*"

We, salt and sea and dust of galaxy, branched from testis and ovary, sex and soul, our origins lost to daylight's thin trace, the gunk and spunk of centuries dimming the information DNA has held hidden for eons and eras, every lumen of insight thinner and paler with each furcation back to the successive prior unions of sperm and egg. We know nothing of faces or hands, the depth of footprint or curve of spine, how the eyes of our antecedents held glittering flakes of arthropod and granite, flecks of carbon, infoldings of protein, whether each coupling was abetted by atoms recognizing other atoms as mirrored turns of advancing or receding spiral nebulae, by organic and inorganic molecules awakening to recall the repetition of previous intricate fits and thread twists of particle and wave, complicated patterning of Fibonaccian twines and Borromean rings. Yet we two, who came together through the weft and warp and frazzled rope, fray and splintered graft, the miscellaneous and multifarious paths of fate, fortune and happen-stance, to find one another and bind, repeat and share what we swear is unique to us, what will be unique to our children, what we alone contain and comprise, what generations of beings and stars have stowed within us, packed so well and soundly for our voyage, have arrived, here and now, to wed.

VI
"There are dead stars that still shine because their light is trapped in time. Where do I stand in this light, which does not strictly exist?"
— Don DeLillo

Repose

"climbing down
feeling the avalanche
in each stone"
— Tom Williamson

Fellfield slope,
precipitous jumble—
stumble at your own
peril; nudge the wrong
round stone, misjudge
the angle of repose—
close out your account,
your life forfeit: no
amount of prayer,
no sufficient number
of lit candles will bring
you out from under
the stony slope, reset
the rumble of your end,
eliminate your new role:
pebbly prole, stony soul,
most current addition
to fellfield's toll.

Cold Spell

When the low descends like judgment
on Great Slave Lake up there,

and icy snow blows, howls, and rends
the lair of the snowshoe hare,

the Canada lynx loses the scent,
belly empty as his stare.

When mongrel hordes of northern winds
plunder Fort Smith and Calgary,

Lord forgive me all my sins;
I put my faith in Thee.

When Blue Northers storm the border
and Bismarck makes the news,

frigid chaos murders order,
blizzards white out the view,

and the Polar Vortex marauder,
takes aim at me and you,

then I'll find my child-like faith again,
as strong as strong can be.

Lord forgive all my sins;
I put my faith in Thee.

B&O

"rusted train tracks…
a young maple
turning red"
——Betty Drevniok

The lullaby of the B&O——
no longer calms children
on Christmas Eve, leadens
the eyes of insomniacs,
lulls to blessed unconsciousness
widowers newly wide-eyed
in a room suddenly empty
that had always before
been shared, no longer soothes
laid-off miners or farmers
praying for three more nights
without rain, or young women
counting how many days late
their time of the month,
young men wondering
if their marriage proposal
will be accepted, ——
lingers on only in the dreams
of those of us who once laid awake
half the night just to croon along.

Don't

"…I don't march. I'm the one who leaps."
—Jericho Brown

just

break

step.

Leap

the arch-legged,

reaching bound

of *premier danseur*

hovering at the apex

of his trajectory.

Be steeplechase steed,

legs and belly tangent

to parabolic arc.

Become the geometry

of sonnets, sonatas,

the draftsman's inked contour,

the airliner's streamline,

Jupiter's rising path

against the soaring

September sky.

Evolution's copy editor

misses the occasional
typo, allows the bot fly,
the deer tick, the oak
mite to sneak by—
perhaps to test
our attention span—

keeps us awake
bragging how
he slipped *Trypanosoma*
past our sleepily
nodding heads,

then, to relieve
the boredom, watches
our reaction
to the question mark
of the hookworm.

Sanctification

"…my bones atremble at your tabernacle
of rhythm and blues"
—Barbara Hamby, "Vex Me"

Blues arose from the sanctimony
of Sundays, the sins of Saturday nights,
the tavern, the tabernacle, the barroom
and brothel, soul immortal, body
tempestuous, bone and flesh, hair and nail,
plush cash, flush of passion, rattle of dice,
fling of feet, ring of laughter, sigh
of satisfaction, preacher's roar, gospel
chorus's soar, children's shouts, Jim Crow
louts, Whites Only, harmonica's lonely
midnight moon-spite freight train wail.

Last Snow of Winter

"…in that distant gray where day meets night."
—B. H. Fairchild, "The Gray Man"

night met day this morning
as a gradual brightening,
the grays and whites honest,
forthright, backlit a bit more
with each passing moment,
so that the snowflakes
became lost in a distant and granular mist,

whereas, at three a.m.
they had been aborning
from grayness, all the city
glow's luminance trapped
in the short distance bound
by white amorphous ground shapes
and lowering cloud-like snow whorls,

but now that stage ceiling has been lifted
by light to another half its prior height
and the softened geometry of house
and street have become rounded
and smoothed and the flakes smaller
and more rapid and the wind scurries after them,

the whole storm now funneling
between white sky and white
ground as the day chases
the night off to the increasingly
frantic staccato whisks of icy crystals:
presto, *accelerando*,
prestissimo

Moments

Today bluish shadows streaked icy snow,
the breeze was brisk as lemon is taut,
and to brown paper leaves the sun bestowed
gilt edges and folds. Such riches, I thought,
should be shared and saved, so here they are,
tucked into this poem, into my heart,
things you wouldn't have to go very far
to see for yourself, so why even start?

Look out your window, cant your view,
gather the everyday sights you see,
the ones that will then be imbued
with all the love you hold for me
send me a sonnet comprised of these things—
the simple moments your day's unfolding brings.

A Simple Exercise

It should be easy as cut and paste.
But in midwinter's florid expanse
our fingers are too cold for typing,
for holding pen.

We should be able to pluck the words
from our minds' eyes, fling them
with shakes of our heads onto
one another's visual neurons: pursue
the practice of psionic prosody.

If it was snowing, we might flick flakes
telepathically, icy mental hieroglyphics
cast onto the blank pages of each other's
frontal lobes.

But here in the day's deepening dusk,
let us look instead into one another's pupils—
optic nerves flaring metaphors like halogen
filaments, lyricism mapping the fluorescent
boundaries of undiscovered countries directly
from our convoluted brains onto the warped
spheroid planets of our January eyes.

Suppose

Suppose God hadn't set this whole thing
in motion after all? I mean, suppose
that He instead chose it from a bunch
of spare universes in some stockpile
that He found at *The Thrifty God's
Wholesale Universe Outlet Store*,

a big-box warehouse out along
the freeway after He had just happened to see
the *EXIT HERE* sign as He was trying out
His trick of assembling Himself into
a V-16 Ferrari with hyper overdrive
and 32 valves with heated and cooled

Corinthian Leather seats, and He
had been timing 0-100 acceleration
runs and fine-tuning His *other-self-as-automatic-
braking-system* to keep His V-16 self skid-free
in a sudden stop, and suppose He got distracted,
as He was often likely to do,

what with His infinities of days
that kind of ran into one another,
you know, as if they all kind of blurred
into a barely countable infinity
of Tuesdays, not the rough Mondays
after the wild weekend,

not hump days with all their potential,
just ordinary old Tuesdays
with nothing on the old calendar
(Wait a minute, He thought,
Have I made part of Me into
one of those calendar thingies yet?),
and as He pulled into what looked to be

a ten-acre parking lot, filled with other
parts of Himself Who had turned *Themselves*
into 18-wheelers (One had gone to 32-wheels,
and He briefly thought of trying
to one-up *that Version* of Himself

and to turn His *Current Self*
into a 48-wheeler), He just went in
and bought *this* old Universe,
as-is, rode hard and stabled wet,
cash on the barrelhead.
I mean, just Suppose!

Venus

owns the morning sky,
blatant, blaringly bright
diva planet, the moon's
chief wife, obscuring the rest
of the night harem: (even
Spica—enticing, whirling,
double-star-hip-jewel of Virgo,
the closest competition, but
still a lesser odalisque despite
her dizzying galactic dance).
Moon stares, waning-crescent-
grin, agog at the sight.

Pilgrim

I want to go broadside to the world—
Baltimore Clipper heeled hard
on Atlantic waves, Arctic tern
wheeling through sea spume,
Monarch butterfly glorifying tailwinds
with orange and black fluttering.

I want to float the air's currents:
waft on spirals of thermals painted
by pointillist plumes of pollen; skirt
the gusts of cold fronts, buoy like branches,
like a ballerina's arms, lift like leaves,
like her lithe fingers.

Let me become water droplets
that make visible the patterns
of the world's creatures breathing: the warm
outrush of moist clouds from lungs,
the seeping absorption of carbon dioxide
into the stomata of leaf veins.

Let me ribbon with the intricate
scrolling and rolling of air
in the wake of a distance runner,
roll and bob on the serpentine pattern
of vortices trailing from a woodpecker's
undulating wings.

Let me be a tree-woven hedgerow,
windbreak of Osage orange and red cedar—
my kiting branches broadside to the prairie storm,
straining roots anchoring against everything
the world pushes my way.

VII

"There are two ways of spreading light... To be the candle, or the mirror that reflects it."
—Edith Wharton

Us

Your attention is my poultice,
balm from the crockery, the nectary,
the immanent grace of your soul,
the Gondwanan breadth of your being.

You embellish me, bequeath to me
the honeydew, the tallow, the syllogism
of your inner self. I am chuff,
facile, inchoate without you.

If you would cloister with me,
the world's distractions would
swarm and churn to no avail
outside the binary star of us.

Discourse

"Along the branches of our silence hang our words."
—Vassar Miller, "The Tree of Silence"

The words form,
rounded as apples,
as oblong pears suddenly
succulent, the fleshy home
of pips, of seedling insights,
ideas of future generations
of thoughts and proposals yet
unsaid, but pregnant with years
of considered cogitation to come,
misunderstandings avoided, loves
never lost, brilliant discourses
instigated by foliferous buds,
by orange leaves of words
all strung, curled, intricately
scalloped by the clenched
teeth, the coiled tongue
of silence.

Central Heat

The cat knows—
has staked out
all the best hot-
air vents, lies
in his own dry sauna,
dreams that he
traverses warm
Mediterranean
shores, basks in
his own *leveche*,
his own *sirocco*,
his own *xaloc*,
the furnace-wind ruffling
his long stomach hair
like a Berber's tunic,
that he smells savory
ahriche of sheep, crusty
pastilla of squab. His
stomach rumbles.
Winter drifts on,
outside his notice.

Perception

"Ours is an awful awareness,
filled with itch and wonder."
—Albert Goldbarth, "Perception Poem"

Itch and wonder,
fletch, let fly,
tear asunder,
tear up and cry.

Scratch and ponder,
torch aflare,
caramelize flan—
her favorite fare.

Bleed and flounder,
pound the floor.
She loved you once.
Try once more.

Silverfish

"brushing silverfish out of a notebook of poems"
—Al Ortolani, "Scrooge"

Dog-eared notebooks,
ink-smudged pages,
revisions, second looks,
quiet moments, rages,

erasure impressions,
ideas rethought,
assertions, questions,
words scratched out,

tears or raindrops
crumbs of food
slow starts, rapid stops,
stilted, fluid,

random jottings,
cramped cursive,
blobs, blottings,
boring, immersive,

excerpts, quotes,
snips of phrases,
worries, gloats,
habits, phases,

moments, days,
or months ago,
goings, stayings,
words ebb, worlds flow.

At the Front of Class

"I know nothing of limestone's patience…"
—Traci Brimhall, "*En Plein Aire*"

The patience of limestone,
the angry glow of lava's spume,
the stressed-out tensity of basalt
neither you nor I can comprehend,
although we know the dark, intense
scowl of coal reminds us of a certain
black-clad nun tapping her foot
while we faced the blackboard,
as uncertain about least common
denominators as she was about
patience, about grace.

The Prodigal's Siblings Speak

Why bend a knee in obeisance
when you don't believe in penance,
when you enter these walls in all your arrogance?

Mutter your pious utterance?
Sooth us with your sibilance?
Look at us askance?

Don't you see the reason for our petulance?
Why should we offer tolerance?
The broken bread of sustenance?

Shall we count out the abundance
of your faults? Dalliance?
Dissonance? Extravagance?

Observe our resonance!
See our allegiance
to one another, our obvious endurance!

Did we shout out "Good riddance!"
when you left? Of course! And didn't we dance?
Had we ever felt such buoyance?

Do we believe your hurting stance?
Are your tears of any relevance?
Do you know you are a nuisance?

Do we believe your repentance?
Do you think we're all in a trance?
Do you see any hesitance?

Why cross yourself? Obeisance?
Why nod when told your penance?
Why darken this door once more with your arrogance?

Hand

Your hand alights,
bird-like, on
my shoulder,
then, all lift gone
from folded wing,
fingers, palm,
a bare fraction
of love's depth,
settle.

I envelop the role
of branch haven,
await nesting,
rested warmth,
contented roosting,
the essential fledgling calm
of familiar touch.

Barn Swallows

Gesso sky today—
swallows dry brush it
with their wings.
They float on
your pupils,
swim the vitreous
humor, dive into
retinal depths, clog
the brightness,
jam your neural
pathways—
those afterimages
the only trails
they leave against
the trackless gray.

A Fish Stew or Two

"…shellfish in coolers, boiling
and bouillabaissing"
——Sharon Olds, "Attempted Banquet"

A bouillabaisse and a cioppino
are two sides of a coin, one of those
made by diffusion bonding stainless
steel and copper, like the pot one might
simmer them in, their respective sauces
bubbling against shell and carapace,
suffusing translucent halibut with whiteness,
taming the live pink of salmon flank
to flaked pastel, turning shrimp and crab claw
brilliant red, prying open mussel's sleek
black shell, oyster's crinkled grizzle, scallop's
limey corrugated lips to reveal the plump meat
within, lying all a-jumble in respective broths,
fish stock or tomato base, geyser hot,
beside crusty bread and fine fierce wine
and appetites unbounded.

Adjacence

"beyond the peripheral picture of us
there is absence"—E. Peterson

What's wrong with being
essential but never central,
being the sultry spice of rind,
never the saccharine plush
of pulp, the tapered oval
translucence of eggshell, never
the vivid sphere of yolk?

You will always be peripheral
to a lover's macular degeneration,
viewed aslant by those with billiard eyes,
banking off glancing blows into side pockets.

You will always be among the thousands
of extras, the movie set's background
to the stars, the photograph's bokeh,
the fringe, the border, the frame
that constitutes the world's abundant
adjacence.

Notes & Acknowledgments

"Adjacence" first appeared in *River City Poetry*, Fall 2019 Issue.

"After Leaf Raking" first appeared in *I-70 Review*, 2021. It is an homage to Robert Frost, after one of my favorites of his poems, "After Apple Picking."

"Age Tries to Recall Youth's Departure" first appeared in *River City Poetry*, Spring 2021 Issue.

"Barbara Hamby Embraces the Swedish Word *Mångata*"— first appeared in *MacQueen's Quinterly*, Issue 5, Oct. 2020. The Barbara Hamby quote in the epigraph is from "Craft Tip #5: Choosing Your Words" (Pp. 40-42 in *The Practicing Poet: Writing Beyond the Basics*, by Diane Lockward, Terrapin Books, 2018). The poem referenced by Hamby is "The Dream of the Dacha," from her book, *Bird Odyssey* (Pitt Poetry Series, University of Pittsburgh Press, 2018). "*Mångata*" – is pronounced "Moun-ga-ta" - literally "moon road" from the Swedish "*Måne*" (moon) [pronounced "Mouh uh neh"] and "*gata*" (street) [pronounced "goh-ah-ta"]. The word "*nubbe*" is pronounced "new-beh" and denotes schnapps as well as the glass used to drink them. "*Akvavit*" is pronounced "aw-kwa-veet," and is a Scandinavian spirit distilled from potatoes and grain. "*Skål*" is pronounced "Sko-awl." The letter "å" is pronounced "oo-ah."

"Central Heat" first appeared in *MacQueen's Quinterley*, Issue 1, Jan. 2020. A *leveche* is a local wind that affects southeastern Spain, a *sirocco* is a warm south wind that occurs in Algeria and the Levant. The word *xaloc* is a Catalan name for the *sirocco*. Each of these is a hot, dry wind of tropical continental origin which occurs in the Mediterranean region. *Ahriche* is tripe wrapped around a stick and cooked over hot coals. *Pastilla* is a traditional Moroccan meat pie.

"Chiaroscuro (After Caravaggio's 'Sacrifice of Abraham')" – The image used is in the Public Domain, Downloaded from WikiMedia Commons, August 2022. Link: https://commons.wikimedia.org/wiki/File:Sacrifice_of_Isaac-Caravaggio_(c._1603).jpg

"Clarity" first appeared in *The COOP*, Sept. 2021.

"The Color of Blessings" first appeared in *MacQueen's Quinterley*, Issue 5, Oct. 2020.

"The Currency of His Light," after Claude Monet's series of *Houses of Parliament* impressionist paintings, first appeared in *The Ekphrastic Review*, Nov. 23, 2020. Image used is in the Public Domain, Downloaded from WikiMedia Commons, Aug. 2022. Link: https://commons.wikimedia.org/wiki/File:The_Houses_of_Parliament_(Effect_of_Fog).JPG

"Declarative," which first appeared in *River City Poetry*'s Fall 2019 issue, is an ekphrastic poem inspired by photographer Kathrin Swoboda's award-winning pictures of a red-winged blackbird singing on a cold morning, his breath condensing and glistening in the sun's warm light. See her photographs at
https://mymodernmet.com/red-winged-blackbird-kathrin-swoboda/.

Epigraph for this book: (*"Sometimes a piece of the sun burned like a coin between my hands."— Pablo Neruda*) is from Neruda's poem, "Clenched Soul."

Epigraph for Chapter I: (*"When I consider how my light is spent, Ere half my days, in this dark world and wide…" — John Milton*) is from his Sonnet 19, from the book *Poems 1673*.

Epigraph for Chapter II: (*"I don't paint people and things; I paint the way light reacts to people and things."* — *Harley Brown*) is a quote widely attributed to contemporary Canadian artist Harley Brown.

Epigraph for Chapter III: (*"I have seized the light. I have arrested its flight."* —*Louis Daguerre*) is attributed to Daguerre in *National Geographic*, Oct. 1989, pg. 530.

Epigraph for Chapter IV: (*"To light a candle is to cast a shadow."* — *Ursula K. LeGuin*) is from her 1968 book, *A Wizard of Earthsea* (Parnassus Press).

Epigraph for Chapter V: (*"Look at light and admire its beauty. Close your eyes, and then look again: what you saw is no longer there; and what you will see later is not yet."* —*Leonardo da Vinci*) Widely attributed to da Vinci, although I could find no specific citation.

Epigraph for Chapter VI: (*"There are dead stars that still shine because their light is trapped in time. Where do I stand in this light, which does not strictly exist?"* — *Don DeLillo*) can be found on p. 178 of DeLillo's novel, *Cosmopolis* (Scribner, 2003).

Epigraph for Chapter VII: (*"There are two ways of spreading light… To be the candle, or the mirror that reflects it."* —*Edith Wharton*) is from her poem, "Vesalius in Zante. (1564)" *North American Review* 175 (Nov. 1902): 625-631.

"Evolution's copy editor…" first appeared in *Chiron Review* (2020). *Trypanosoma* is a microscopic parasite transmitted to humans by the tsetse fly that causes African sleeping sickness.

"A Father Who Lives Longer Than His Son (A Villanelle)" first appeared in *River City Poetry*, Spring 2021 Issue.

"Forever" first appeared as a flash historical fiction piece in *The Ekphrastic Review*, 15 November, 2021. It has been recast here as an ekphrastic poem. Quotes in the poem are from *Letter 678* from

Vincent van Gogh to Wilhelmina van Gogh, 9 & 16 Sept. 1888. [http://vangoghletters.org/vg/letters/let678/letter.html] "The Cafe Terrace on the Place du Forum" was the first of van Gogh's starry night works. It was followed by: "Starry Night Over the Rhone" (*Musee d'Orsay*, painted Sept. 1888, "Portrait of Eugene Boch" (*Musee d'Orsay*, painted Sept. 1888), and "Starry Night" (MOMA, painted June 1889). Image used is in the Public Domain, Downloaded from WikiMedia Commons, August 2022. Link: https://commons.wikimedia.org/w/index.php?search=The+Cafe+Terrace+on+the+Place+du+Forum&title=Special:MediaSearch&go=Go&type=image.

"Funereal" first appeared in *The Shining Years: Poems about Aging* (2021, Blue Wild Indigo Productions, Gary J. Lechliter, Editor). The epigraph is from Jenny Molberg's poem, "Our Lady of the Rio Grande."

"A Golden Shovel Poem After Li Po's 'Drinking in Moonlight'" - The lines of this poem begin with the words (or an approximation of the words) that comprise the first five lines of Li Po's poem (as translated by David Young in *Five Tang Poets*, 1990, Oberlin College Press): "I sit with my wine jar / among flowers / blossoming trees / no one to drink with / well there's the moon…"

"The House Awakens" is a sonnet that uses *antimetabole*, a form of *chiasmus*; the words ending the first seven lines are used, in reverse order, to end the last seven. The words were selected from Jeanine Hathaway's book, *Long after Lauds* (2019, Slant, Eugene, OR).

"Hummingbirds" first appeared in *MacQueen's Quinterley*, Issue 11, January 2022. The allusions in the second stanza of this poem include: Gumby—an American clay animation character, created and modeled by Art Clokey in the early 1950s. Wallace and Gromit— are British stop motion comedy characters created by Nick Park of Aardman Animations. *The Blue Angel* (German: *Der blaue Engel*)—a 1930 German film directed by Josef von Sternberg and starring Marlene Dietrich, and Emil Jannings.

"Lexicon" first appeared in *The COOP*, Oct. 2021.

"Light lies on water…" first appeared in *The Midwest Quarterly*, Summer Edition, 2022.

"Mark" first appeared in *River City Poetry*, Fall 2019.

"Nature and Nurture" was inspired by and modeled after Betsy Sholl's poem, "Genealogy," which first appeared in *Field: Contemporary Poetry and Poetics,* #81, Fall, 2009, Oberlin College Press, which has been a source of inspiration for many other writers before me.

"Poem Written on the First Anniversary of My Son's Death" first appeared in the June 2020 Special Edition of *River City Poetry* and was written during the height of the 2020 COVID pandemic; my son Mark died unexpectedly in 2019, a month prior to his 57th birthday, apparently of a broken heart, after nursing his wife, Virginia, through the last year of her death from lung and brain cancer. His death was nearly one year after hers. Title after Jay Hopler's "Poem Written on the First Anniversary of My Father's Death."

"Prothalamion" first appeared in *MacQueen's Quinterly*, Issue 6, 2021.

"Pyramidal" was inspired by Julian Talamantez Brolaski's "Pyramidal, Its Certain Form," which appeared in *Poetry Magazine*, Dec. 2018.

"Rust Belt" first appeared in *River City Poetry* Fall 2019, as "Oxidation".

"Sea Sprites in Flight" first appeared in *River City Poetry*, Spring 2021 Issue. Image used is in the Public Domain, Downloaded from WikiMedia Commons, Aug. 2022. Link:

https://commons.wikimedia.org/w/index.php?title=File:Fitzgerald,_Sea_Sprites_in_Flight.jpg&oldid=191291361

"Shores" first appeared in *MacQueen's Quinterly*, Issue #9, 2021.

"A Simple Exercise" was inspired by a twenty-minute writing exercise of the same title in the book *The Poet's Companion* (1997, W.W. Norton & Co.) by Kim Addonizio and Dorianne Laux.

"Starlings: Ode to Murmuration" first appeared in *MacQueen's Quinterley*, Issue 11, Jan. 2022.

"Symphony Below the Threshold of Hearing" first appeared in *MacQueen's Quinterly*, Issue #9, 2021.

"Us" first appeared in Vol. 5, Issue 3 (2020) of *Mockingheart Review*.

"Walking always goes forward" is an epistolary poem that first appeared in *Enduring Puberty: annual volume of literary, visual, and epistolary art*, Issue #2: pp. 52-53, June 30, 2019. The first photo is one of the author as a child taken by his father at the front porch of his first home, the second a cell-phone photo of that house taken by the author some 70+ years later. The word *DeLorean* refers to the sports car (manufactured by The DeLorean Motor Company from 1981-1983) that is modified into a time machine in the movie "Back to The Future" (Amblin Entertainment, 1985) and "McFly" to the name of the movie's protagonist, Marty McFly (played by actor Michael J. Douglas).

"The Way Night's Lapidary Light Burnishes Your Skin" first appeared in *MacQueen's Quinterly*, Issue 6, 2021, and is dedicated to my wife, Patricia Beckemeyer.

"We All Breathe" first appeared in the June 2020 Special Edition of *River City Poetry*.

"When they last bloomed…" was inspired by the William Matthews' line in the epigraph, which brought to my mind Walt Whitman's elegy for Abraham Lincoln's assassination. I also drew on these lines from Whitman: "When lilacs last in my dooryard bloom'd"; "every leaf a miracle"; "the tally of my soul".

"Whirl" first appeared in *The COOP,* Feb. 15, 2021.

The Author

Roy Beckemeyer of Wichita has BS, MS, and Ph.D. degrees in engineering from St. Louis University, Wichita State University, and the University of Kansas, respectively. He retired from a 30-year career at Boeing in research and development, airplane design, and executive management. He has read and written poetry since high school; his post-retirement poetry has been widely published in literary journals and anthologies. He has four previous poetry collections in print: his most recent is *Mouth Brimming Over* (2019, Blue Cedar Press); *Stage Whispers* (2018, Meadowlark Books) won the 2019 Nelson Poetry Book Award; *Amanuensis Angel* (2018, Spartan Press) assembled ekphrastic poems inspired by depictions of angels in works of modern art; *Music I Once Could Dance To* (2014, Coal City Press) was a 2015 Kansas Notable Book. He is co-editor of several poetry anthologies, including *Kansas Time+Place: An Anthology of Heartland Poetry* (2017, Little Balkans Press, with Caryn Mirriam-Goldberg). He won the 2016 Kansas Voices award, and his poetry has been nominated for Pushcart and Best of the Net awards; his prose poem, "Words for Snow," was selected for *Best Small Fictions 2019*. He and his wife, Pat, celebrated their 60th-anniversary in 2021. In his spare time, he has edited two scientific journals and conducted and published research on the Paleozoic insect fossils of Kansas, Oklahoma, and Alabama. Visit his author's page at: https://royjbeckemeyer.com/.

www.ingramcontent.com/pod-product-compliance
Lightning Source LLC
Chambersburg PA
CBHW071854070526
44583CB00016B/1679